Chris,

Happy &
to a special fri
you've helped to start
me on my journey of
recovery serenity
by your giving of
yourself.

Love & peace,
Susan

HAZELDEN® MEDITATIONS

REFLECTIONS

ON

GIVING,
RECEIVING,
AND
SERENITY

GIVING
RECEIVING
OUR HIGHER POWER
SERENITY

VERONICA RAY

WINGS BOOKS
New York • Avenel, New Jersey

Editor's Note:
Hazelden Educational Materials offers a variety of information on chemical dependency and related areas. Our publications do not necessarily represent Hazelden or its programs, nor do they officially speak for any Twelve Step organization.

This book was originally published in separate volumes under the titles:
Giving, copyright © 1990, Hazelden Foundation
Receiving, copyright © 1990, Hazelden Foundation
Our Higher Power, copyright © 1990, Hazelden Foundation
Serenity, copyright © 1990, Hazelden Foundation

This edition contains the complete and unabridged texts of the original editions. They have been completely reset for this volume.

This 1996 edition is published by Wings Books, a division of Random House Value Publishing, Inc., 40 Engelhard Avenue, Avenel, New Jersey 07001, by arrangement with the Hazelden Foundation.

Wings Books and colophon are trademarks of Random House Value Publishing, Inc.

Random House
New York • Toronto • London • Sydney • Auckland

Printed and bound in the United States of America

Library of Congress Cataloging-in-Publication Data
Ray, Veronica.
    Reflections on giving, receiving, and serenity / Veronica Ray.
        p.   cm. — (Hazelden meditation series)
    Originally published in 1990 as 4 booklets by the Hazelden Foundation.
    Contents: Giving — Receiving — Our higher power — Serenity.
    ISBN 0-517-15023-9
    1. Twelve-step programs—Meditations.   2. Devotional calendars.
I. Title.   II. Series.
BL624.5.R38   1996
291.4'3—dc20   95-42626
                                                    CIP

8   7   6   5   4   3   2   1

Contents

GIVING   1

RECEIVING   35

OUR HIGHER POWER   69

SERENITY   103

GIVING

INTRODUCTION

. . . in truth it is life that gives unto life—
while you, who deem yourself a giver, are but
a witness.

—Kahlil Gibran

Spiritual energy flows *through* us, not from us.
If we let it, this creative energy can use us as channels to flow out into the world. We allow this energy to flow through us in every way we give to
other people, other living things, and the earth.

Our own particular bodies, minds, abilities, and
talents shape and focus the energy flowing through
us. When we sing or play a musical instrument, we
turn the energy into music. When we take care of
others who are sick or injured, we turn the energy
into healing. When we put a seed in the ground, we
turn the energy into a living, growing plant. There
are countless ways in which we channel the loving,
life-giving energy of the universe.

We are all giving in this way, all the time. It
doesn't require money or any special knowledge or
skills. We each contribute in our own ways. Many
of us simply don't recognize all the wonderful ways
we channel positive energy. Some of us feel afraid
or unable to give much. But we can all begin opening up more and more, recognizing and allowing
positive energy to flow freely through us.

The more we open ourselves to the flow of
spiritual energy, the more we are able to give. This
keeps the energy moving, blessing the entire world,

including ourselves. So the more we give, the more we receive.

We *all* have a great deal to give. And we are all needed to give whatever we can to make the world as good as it can be. In the words of Henry Wadsworth Longfellow, "Give what you have. To someone, it may be better than you dare to think."

OUTFLOWING

Sometimes, we don't feel we have much to give others. We may be struggling financially. We may feel too tired, physically and emotionally, to add even one more activity to our busy day.

But we all have a great deal to give, whatever our circumstances. We can listen when someone needs to talk. We can call someone who may be lonely. We can overlook other people's faults and mistakes. We can forgive people who have hurt us. We can teach a skill or share our knowledge. We can offer a smile or an encouraging word to someone who needs it. We can cheer and applaud for others.

We have all our thoughts, attitudes, and actions to give the world. All we have to do is reach into the best part of ourselves and let it flow outward.

Every day I have many chances to give something to others.

DOING

~~~~~~~~~

We read, think, pray, and meditate to find our deep inner spirituality and connection to our Higher Power. But eventually, we must put our knowledge, wisdom, and serenity into *action*.

The step from thinking to doing may be difficult for us to take. We may fear failure, rejection, or ridicule. We may remember only our past mistakes. We may have little experience doing anything when we're not influenced by outside sources.

But we really don't know what we can do until we try. We have inner resources we may have never used before. We can learn to trust our inner resources and let our spirit guide us. Our spirituality is not an escape from the real world. Instead, it helps us cope and perform better in our daily lives. It guides and encourages us to the best possible action.

I express my highest spiritual self in all my actions.

Responsible Speech

Before we speak, do we think about the effects our words might have on others? Gossip, rudeness, lying, and breaking confidences can easily slip into our daily speech. We may use words that trigger negative reactions in others. And when they're offended, we may think they're being unreasonable—we didn't mean any harm.

But regardless of our intentions, our words can harm, and we need to use them responsibly. In speech, we're responsible for respecting other people's feelings, integrity, and privacy. We're responsible for our own honesty and truthfulness.

Becoming sensitive to the power of our words doesn't mean we can never disagree with others or stand up for ourselves. It means taking the same responsibility for our speech as we do for all our other actions.

I am responsible for using speech positively.

True Listening

M. Scott Peck wrote, ". . . true listening is love in action." When we truly listen to others, we're telling them they matter, they're important, and we care. True listening means setting aside all other activities and thoughts. It means turning off the television, putting down the newspaper, and sitting still.

When we offer someone the gift of true listening, we let go of our assumptions and preconceptions. We open ourselves to whatever they want to say. We don't jump right in with our judgments or opinions. We may nod occasionally, or let them know we understand. We may ask questions for clarity, or we may just keep quiet.

We may learn more in a few minutes of true listening than hours of discussing or arguing. And we can grow closer to others than we may ever have thought possible.

I offer others the gift of true listening.

Part of Nature

We use nature for our comfort, convenience, and survival. We are dependent upon nature, but it is also dependent upon us. How we affect the living earth affects ourselves, other people, and future generations.

It's easy to forget our place in the natural world. But we can begin remembering by looking at it closely, through childlike eyes. We can look at mountains, oceans, islands, rivers, trees, lakes, and flowers—smell them, touch them, listen to them. We can watch animals, birds, and fish, especially in their natural environments. As we look at photographs of earth taken from space, we can see it as one whole living thing.

We can take responsibility for nature just as we take responsibility for our own bodies and homes. Through our attitudes and actions, we can love nature, ourselves, others, and all future generations.

I am part of this beautiful and fragile planet.

Our Example

As adults, we often think of ourselves as examples for children, but we are also examples for each other. Every act of courage—whether saving a life, starting a new job, or recovering from an addiction—inspires others. Every act of love—from a generous donation of time or money to a simple kind word—encourages more of the same.

We can sow the seeds of love, courage, peacefulness, generosity, tolerance, compassion, hope, honesty, forgiveness, and joy. We can plant images of responsibility, integrity, and dignity. Whatever we do, we can spread these kernels of positive energy. Just as Johnny Appleseed changed the landscape of the country by planting apple orchards, we can affect the world. It doesn't require fame or prestige, but grows from the seeds of example we plant.

I send the best example I can into the world.

RELATIONSHIPS

Our relationships with others are wonderful opportunities for us to learn and grow. They offer unique challenges and chances to share ourselves. Each person who comes into our lives brings special needs. Every relationship we have is important in its own way.

Each of our relationships offers different opportunities for us to give our time, attention, assistance, encouragement, understanding, acceptance, and forgiveness. They all give us the chance to find out how much we have to share.

Giving all we can to others in our relationships doesn't mean ignoring or neglecting our own needs. One of the best gifts we can give others is our health and happiness. We can't give what we don't have; we can't keep what we won't give away.

My relationships are opportunities for me to learn, grow, and share.

LABOR OF LOVE

Physical labor can give us a tremendous sense of satisfaction. We often talk about feeling "a good kind of tired" after strenuous work. The products of this kind of labor are usually visible, touchable, tangible. And this makes it very *real* to us.

The fruits of our labor rarely affect us alone. A clean window is a joy to look through. An orderly room is pleasant to be in. A beautiful lawn or garden blesses everyone who sees it, as well as the earth in which it grows.

Whether you're shoveling snow or building an ice sculpture . . . refinishing furniture or loading it on a truck . . . whether you're giving birth to a building, bridge, meal, flower bed, work of art, or baby—your labor can be filled with love. When your labor is filled with love, pride, joy, and purpose, it is a blessing to the whole world.

All my labor is filled with love.

The Golden Rule

The Golden Rule is the most basic requirement of harmonious human relations. But we're often confused about its meaning. If we're kind to someone will they automatically treat us kindly? Experience shows this doesn't necessarily happen. So what's the point?

How we treat others, both in thought and action, is really how we treat ourselves. For example, if we "hate" someone, that feeling is within *us* corroding *our* happiness. If we lie to someone, we're not acting in harmony with *our* inner sense of truth, and this hurts *us*.

Kindness may or may not inspire kindness in return, but hostility, deceit, and harm will definitely return to us in some way. If we treat others with kindness, gentleness, understanding, honesty, and generosity, our reward will be our own inner peace and happiness.

I will treat others as I wish to be treated.

APPRECIATION

Many of us may find it difficult to express our appreciation to others. We can overcome our fears and hesitation by remembering how we feel when we're thanked or complimented. Even if we're shy about receiving other people's appreciation, it does make us feel good.

We can express appreciation for people's talents, work, or success. We can compliment their performances and creations. We can thank them for their assistance, encouragement, companionship, or kindness.

We could make a list of everyone to whom we want to express some form of appreciation. This might include teachers, ministers, friends, relatives, co-workers, or anyone. We can express our appreciation to these people face-to-face, on the phone, or in a note. Developing a habit of expressing our appreciation regularly can enrich all our relationships.

I express my appreciation to others.

HONESTY

Being honest is more than just not lying. It's being faithful to our inner truth. It's acting in harmony with our true beliefs. It's standing up for what we believe is right, and admitting when we're wrong.

Honesty requires that we make our choices carefully, and then take their consequences. We don't blame other people or systems. Honesty is taking responsibility for our attitudes, actions, and lives. We don't have to be perfect. Sometimes we'll make mistakes. But if we are honest about them, each mistake can teach us a valuable lesson.

The honesty we send out into the world can improve all our relationships. It can even inspire honesty in others. If we all tried it, it could change the world.

I act and live honestly.

Making Amends

We all make mistakes sometimes. We sometimes let our fears, doubts, and addictions control our actions. Our old negative tapes may interfere with our new honesty and serenity.

Sometimes, these errors affect other people adversely. But indulging in self-hatred and despair doesn't undo the wrong or help the person we've harmed. We need to forgive ourselves and get on with making amends.

The first step in making amends is admitting our mistake and apologizing. If we are humble and honest with ourselves, our apology will be sincere. Next, we make whatever restitution we can, depending on the situation. Finally, we learn whatever lesson the error contained for us. This will help keep us from repeating the mistake. By making amends we improve all our actions and relationships.

I admit my mistakes and make amends promptly.

THOUGHTFULNESS

Thoughtfulness simply means thinking of others. It means recognizing their humanity, acknowledging their value, and respecting their feelings. It means giving them a little boost when they're down, and celebrating their joy when they're up.

We can all learn to become more thoughtful. Thinking of others feels good and contributes to all our relationships.

We can remember to *keep it simple.* Expensive gifts aren't usually the best way to be thoughtful. What others usually want from us is our attention—some sign that we really see them, hear them, and care for them. A card, a call, a few words of praise or encouragement—these are gifts of thoughtfulness.

I think of others in all my relationships.

GOOD INTENTIONS

Sometimes, with the best intentions, we fail to do good or accidentally cause harm. We may be discouraged by this, and shy away from trying again the next time.

But if our intentions are truly good, their value is never lost. We can learn from our error, make amends, and move on. Good thoughts and intentions reach out and bless the world just as good actions do. All is not lost unless we choose to sink into anger, despair, and self-pity.

Perhaps we can carry out our good intentions in another way. Perhaps we were trying to do good in a situation that was simply out of our control. Whatever the case, we can pray for guidance, wisdom, and serenity. We can accept the lesson with honesty, humility, and gratitude. We can concentrate on the good.

I act on good intentions, and try to learn from the results.

CREATIVE EXPRESSION

Many of us were discouraged early in life from expressing ourselves creatively. Often, we were told by others which things we were "good at" and advised against bothering with the rest. Perhaps we heard things like "boys don't dance," or "girls can't play the saxophone." Or perhaps our families couldn't afford the lessons.

But it's never too late to begin learning to express ourselves creatively. If there's something creative we've always wanted to do, whether it's tap dancing or writing poetry, we can now do it. If there's something we used to enjoy, but stopped, we can now go back to it. Creative expression is a gift, not just for the "talented" few, but for all of us. We share it with each other joyfully, because the joy of sharing is its purpose.

I express myself creatively.

Positive Energy

For an exercise in creative energy, we can roll up a sheet of paper or use the inside of a paper towel roll, and cover it with words, pictures, and other symbols for energy we want to send out into the world. We can choose qualities such as love, peace, joy, understanding, and forgiveness. We could also symbolize the specific contributions we wish to make in areas of our lives. As we do this, we remember that these are not objects, qualities, or achievements we wish to draw to ourselves, but energies we are sending *outward*.

Now, as we hold it in our hands, we can imagine that we *are* a tube. As we feel the positive energy flowing through us and out into the world, we can ask our Higher Power to use us as an open channel through which loving, healing, and creative energy flow. We might now repeat an affirmation such as this line from the prayer of St. Francis of Assisi:

Lord, make me an instrument of your peace.

FORGIVENESS

Forgiveness is a gift we can give another, but it is also one of the greatest gifts we can give ourselves. In releasing others, we too are released from our anger, blame, fear, and self-righteousness.

It may seem difficult to let go of judging, condemning, and retaliation until we realize that they only hurt ourselves. When we value peace, harmony, and happiness, we are ready to forgive.

Forgiveness doesn't require approval or affection, or ever seeing the person again. We just do it, inside our own minds and hearts. We just let go of our anger, fear, and judgments, wishing all good things for everyone. When we can do this, we will be free.

I forgive everyone in my life.

KINDNESS

~~~~

Aesop wrote, "No act of kindness, however small, is ever wasted." Every benevolent action blesses all humanity and returns to us.

Kind actions grow from kind thoughts and attitudes. When we see others as our equals and wish them well, it's easy to be kind. When we take responsibility for our own happiness, we can afford to be kind toward others.

Performing acts of kindness in our daily lives doesn't require money, power, or any special skills. It only requires *empathy*—the recognition of our humanity and the desire to make things a little easier for someone else. Thoughtfulness, helpfulness, compassion, understanding, and gentleness are the hallmarks of human kindness.

I spread kindness in the world, and it returns to me, magnified.

ORDER

Human beings seem naturally pleased by order. We like rhyming words, harmonious sounds, and balanced pictures. We expect a story to have a beginning, middle, and end.

Perhaps chaos offends our eyes, ears, minds, and spirits because order is natural in the universe. From our solar system to our planet to our bodies, nature behaves methodically and consistently. Years, seasons, and days are regular and cyclical. The laws of math and physics are uniform and systematic.

When we mimic nature in all areas of our lives—achieving consistency, balance, regularity, and harmony—we are happier and more peaceful. We can create this order for ourselves and others in our environments and daily schedules. Order isn't confining; it frees us from the stress and strain of chaos.

I arrange my environment and my life in an orderly way.

23

CHOICES

~~~~~

Every day our choices affect other people. We can make responsible choices if we remember to consider the effects they might have. But sometimes we allow our choices to be made by our addictions, fears, doubts, and other people. When our choices aren't in harmony with our spiritual selves, we feel uncomfortable. This discomfort may show itself in anxiety, depression, irritability, or even physical pain or illness.

We can change the way we make our choices. We can analyze as many different possibilities as we can think of. We can ask for guidance from our Higher Power, and remember to consider the effects of our choices on others. When our highest inner selves are in charge of our decision-making, the right choices become clear.

I make all choices from my highest spiritual self.

ATTITUDES

We send not only our actions out into the world, but all our thoughts, beliefs, and attitudes as well. For example, we may say the words 'thank you' many times throughout a day without ever expressing genuine gratitude.

The feeling, or attitude behind our words usually comes through even if we try to hide it. We often express everything from indifference to hostility, while our actual words may appear to be kind. Then, we may even get angry when others respond to our attitude rather than our words.

If we are honest with ourselves, and remember that others are just like us—imperfect, but doing their best—we can maintain a more loving attitude toward them. When our thoughts and beliefs are positive and loving, our actions will be too.

My attitude toward others is positive, accepting, and loving.

Seeing ourselves as part of the larger community reminds us of our responsibility to it. Whatever we create in our lives and environment is part of the world. We contribute all our thoughts, attitudes, and actions to the world around us. No matter who we are, we make a difference.

We can begin right now, today, adding to the world's love, peace, beauty, understanding, forgiveness, and health by taking care of our own little corner of it. Then perhaps we can reach out a bit farther than we're used to.

No one else can tell us what sort of service to perform for our community. We each contribute in our own unique way. Our Higher Power will guide us. We just need to remember, we do make a difference.

I can make a positive contribution to the world every day.

LOVE

We may find it difficult to understand advice to love everyone. Sometimes we have enough trouble just loving our families and close friends.

The problem is in defining the word *love*. We often think of love as *super-like*. We believe that if we like someone enough, it becomes love. This is a conditional relationship that we fall into and out of depending on how the other person looks, acts, treats us, and what we believe about them.

But there is another kind of love. It's universal and *un*conditional. It doesn't depend on anything about the other person. It doesn't have anything to do with *liking* them. It simply means accepting them, recognizing their humanity and spirituality, and wishing for them only peace, happiness, health, and all good things. When we learn to love everyone this way, our happiness will be guaranteed.

I can love all people.

TRADE-OFFS

What are we willing to sacrifice our happiness for? Is it more important for us to be right or happy? Is it better to feel angry or calm? Whenever we choose anger, hostility, or self-righteousness, we sentence ourselves to misery and pain.

But whatever happens outside us, we can respond with serenity. It may not be our first, automatic response, but we can gently guide ourselves back to it. We can remind ourselves that we have traded our ego's wish to be right for peace and happiness.

Harmonious relations with others make us happier. We don't always have to agree with them, and we never have to allow them to harm us. But we can accept the things we can't change, calmly do whatever we need to do for our well-being, and maintain our peace and happiness.

Nothing is worth trading away my inner peace and happiness.

SHARING

~~~

Many of us were taught to share in ways that seemed like a sacrifice or punishment. Our toys may have been taken from us, or our college fund used for something else in the family. We may never have learned the *joy* of sharing.

How can we share joyfully as long as we think sharing makes us have or be less? Sharing our material goods, time, attention, and selves with others is a joy when we realize that it doesn't deprive us in any way.

We can stop thinking of ourselves as finite containers, holding only so much, and when that's given away, there's nothing left. Instead, we can think of ourselves as channels through which good things flow abundantly and endlessly. When we have faith that there's always plenty more on its way to us, there will be.

Sharing is an expression of faith, love, and joy.

HUMOR

A sense of humor helps us cope with nearly any situation. Humor can help relieve tension between ourselves and others. Used carefully, it can enhance all of our relationships.

But humor is easily misused. There is a difference between keeping a light-hearted sense of humor and putting other people down. There is a difference between being able to laugh at ourselves, in all our humanness, and putting ourselves down.

We can see the funny side of things without disregarding other people's feelings. We can laugh together with pleasure, joy, and delight. We can be like children, naturally enjoying the sheer fun of being alive. When we enjoy life with a healthy sense of humor, everyone around us can feel a little more light-hearted.

I use humor to enjoy life and help others.

CHARITY

Giving to those who may have less than we do is one way of extending ourselves into the world. Cleaning our closets and giving away things we don't need, or donating some of our time or money to a worthy cause keeps positive energy flowing through us.

But sometimes we may feel as if there is no one needier, sicker, lonelier, or poorer than ourselves. These are the times we most need to find the charity in our hearts and extend it outward.

If we have been through a rough experience, we can help others who are going through the same thing. If we can read, we can read to others or teach them to read. And we can always give our prayers for other people's health, happiness, and abundance.

I always have something to give others.

SELF-DISCLOSURE

For many of us, revealing our true selves—our thoughts, feelings, beliefs, and histories—is difficult. We're used to hiding, holding back, protecting ourselves. We may feel confused about who we are. This is when talking things over with someone can be helpful. Saying things out loud often helps clarify them. The viewpoint of a trusted friend or professional can help us see things in a new light.

When guilt, shame, and fear of rejection keep us from self-disclosure, faith and trust are needed. Once we open the door of our true selves to others, we find that the rejection we feared came from ourselves. The understanding and forgiveness of others can inspire self-love. Revealing ourselves, in all our human imperfection, is often the best gift we can give anyone.

I reveal my true self to at least one other person.

GENEROSITY

If we donate a large amount of money to charity only because it's a tax advantage, we're giving only to ourselves. If we give somone a nice gift only because it's expected of us or we expect something in return, we're giving nothing. True generosity can come from only one place—the human heart. The tiniest gift, given from the heart, is priceless. The most lavish present, given for any other reason, is worthless.

We don't have to deprive ourselves. Real generosity doesn't require sacrifice or suffering, great wealth, talent, or success. It only requires a little thought, a little care, a little bit of ourselves.

We can all afford to be generous. We can't afford not to. When we give just to give, joyfully and freely, we learn the supreme truth that giving *is* receiving.

My heart is completely generous and giving.

LOVE AND VISUALIZATION

As we close our eyes, relax, and breathe deeply and slowly, we can imagine someone we love standing before us. This person is very happy and relaxed. Now we see them bathed in a beautiful golden light. This light surrounds and fills them with love, peace, joy, health, and abundance. As we stay with this image, we may tell the person we love them. When we are ready, we let the image dissolve slowly and peacefully.

We can visualize everyone we love in this way, seeing them as completely happy, peaceful, and serene.

We can use this visualization for others as well—particularly those we have trouble getting along with or hold grievances against. We visualize them filled with love, peace, and joy. While we are looking at them in the light, we can tell them we forgive them.

I see everyone in my life filled with light and love.

RECEIVING

INTRODUCTION

Be grateful and believe you deserve the best. You may have more today than you think. And tomorrow may be better than you can imagine.
—Melody Beattie
from *Beyond Codependency*

The positive spiritual energy flowing throughout the universe manifests itself in many ways. If we let it into our lives, it brings love, joy, peacefulness, tranquility, abundance, and all good things and experiences. We can call this *receiving our good*.

It may seem obvious that we all want to receive all the good available in the world. It may seem ridiculous to suggest that we often stop this good from coming into our lives. But we do this in many ways without realizing it.

We block the flow of good when we resent others who we think have more than we do. We block the energy when we believe we don't deserve good. Our fears, doubts, and mistaken beliefs can block the flow of good in our lives. And our past experiences may repeat until we start making changes in ourselves.

We don't receive our good passively. We are active participants. We make it possible for the good to flow freely to us and through us. As we let go of the blocks within ourselves, we open up to the good that can come to us.

Each of us can receive love, happiness, and abundance. We can be grateful for everything in the universe, rejoice in other people's good, and openly receive our own. Everything good can and will come to us, when we let it. Tomorrow may indeed be better than we've ever imagined.

ACTIVE ACCEPTANCE

To receive a pass in football or basketball, we must be open, alert, and ready. We can't just stand by passively waiting for the ball to fall into our hands.

In life, many opportunities can pass us by if we are not open, alert, or ready for them. To be open, we let go of the obstacles we create in our minds; we let go of beliefs that we can't have or don't deserve love, fun, success, happiness, or whatever. Being alert means seeing the good that is there for us. And being ready means being prepared and willing to receive it.

We play an active role in receiving all the good things we want and need for our well-being. When we concentrate our energy on being open, alert, and ready, these good things start flowing into our lives.

I am open, alert, and ready to accept all good things into my life.

Openness

To remove the blocks within us, we must first recognize what they are. Some of us may believe there just isn't enough of the good to go around. Some of us may believe the good is for others, but not for us. We may have grown up with much less love, peace, joy, success, or material comfort than others around us. So we got used to that, and now it feels natural to us— even if we're miserable.

We can understand that what we grew up with doesn't have to be what we're stuck with forever. We can learn that the goodness of the universe is limitless, and our well-being doesn't harm or deprive anyone else. We can begin to love ourselves enough to let good things, feelings, and experiences flow freely into our lives.

I let go of all the blocks to receiving my good.

SEEING THE GOOD

Everything we need for our well-being is always available to us. But we can't always see this. In her book, *Beyond Codependency*, Melody Beattie wrote, "If everything looks black, we've probably got our eyes shut." Fear and doubt shut our eyes. Old, mistaken beliefs shut our eyes.

It's hard to see what we don't believe in. If we're firmly convinced that all people are untrustworthy, we won't recognize a trustworthy person when one comes along. But that doesn't mean there aren't any.

Opening our eyes to the good all around us means letting go of our fears, doubts, and mistaken beliefs. We can't do this all at once, but little by little, one day at a time. As we let in more and more light, our vision becomes clearer, and we discover the good that was there all along.

I open my eyes to the good all around me.

WILLINGNESS

Of course we are all willing to receive good things, feelings, and experiences into our lives. Or are we? Do we really want to have the things we wish for, or do we just want to *want* them? The answer often shows up in our behavior. We may complain and feel sorry for ourselves because we don't have something, but sabotage every opportunity to get it. We may think and say we want all the good the world has to offer, but we don't believe we deserve it or are actually afraid of receiving it.

When we examine our willingness, we may find we're afraid of owing something for everything we receive. Or we may find the things we thought we wanted or needed really wouldn't enhance our well-being at all. When we clear out these fears and delusions, and become truly willing to have all the good, it begins coming to us.

I am willing to acccept the good into my life.

KINDRED SPIRITS

A *kindred spirit* is someone who truly knows us, understands us, and often feels the same way we do. We feel comfortable and safe with this person, and accepted as ourselves. We can say very little to each other and yet share a great deal.

One reason these relationships seem so rare may be that we don't let them unfold. We may play roles with others, never letting them see who we really are. We may give up on relationships at the first misunderstanding. We may not take the time to grow in trust and empathy for each other. We may believe that such relationships just can't happen for us.

But we may have more opportunities to find kindred spirits than we believe. Others may actually have more in common with us than we think possible. In fact, we may *all* be kindred spirits.

I give my relationships the chance to grow.

FORGIVENESS

Sometimes it's hard for us to accept another person's forgiveness. This is usually because we haven't forgiven ourselves. Sometimes we don't yet see what we did wrong, and don't feel we need forgiving.

Whatever the reason, we pass up opportunities to deepen and strengthen our relationships with others when we don't accept their forgiveness. We also lose chances to grow within ourselves. Forgiveness can teach us, heal us, and release us from our prison of guilt and self-hatred.

We can accept other people's forgiveness and learn to forgive ourselves. We can see ourselves more clearly, and begin understanding and learning from our mistakes. We can recognize the strength and love in another's forgiveness, and receive it gratefully.

I accept other people's forgiveness for my mistakes.

HELP

There are times when we willingly accept help from others. If we're badly injured, we go to the emergency room of the nearest hospital and let the staff there treat us. If our plumbing, electricity, or major appliances break down, we usually call in professionals for repair work.

At other times, we may resist accepting the help we need. We may not even want to admit we need help. We may not trust others to give us what we need. We may not believe real help is available.

But help is always available to us. Our families, friends, co-workers, therapists, counselors, ministers, and doctors can help us in various ways. Even strangers can sometimes help us, directly or indirectly. All we have to do is be honest with ourselves, seek the help we need, and accept it when we find it.

I accept all the help I need from others.

SUCCESS

Many of us find it hard to accept success. We deny our accomplishment, crediting other people or luck. We may even feel guilty for succeeding.

When others congratulate or compliment us, we may say, "Oh, it's nothing" or "Anybody could have done it." We may belittle our achievement instead of letting ourselves feel good. We may think our success is a fluke. We don't dare believe compliments and congratulations.

We can free ourselves from this self-defeating pattern. We can accept compliments on our accomplishments, whether a well-cooked meal, a business coup, or a newly learned piece of music. We can learn to simply say, "Thank you." We can accept our successes and the appreciation of others.

I accept and enjoy every success in my life, large and small.

THE POWER OF GOOD

It is easy to find pain, misery, and injustice if we look for it. But it is just as easy to see Good at work in the world. We can see the power of Good in everything from the beauty of nature and the order of the universe to human kindness and generosity. We can see it in the expansion of human knowledge and medical discoveries. We can see it whenever and wherever we look for it with open eyes, minds, and hearts.

Human imperfection can't cancel out the power of Good, which can never be depleted or destroyed. It is always within our reach, anytime, anywhere. It is at work everywhere in the world, all the time. Only if we choose to ignore it, can it escape our attention. We can choose, instead, to let the power of Good light up our vision and strengthen our hope.

I look for and find the power of Good in everything I see.

FRIENDSHIP

Sometimes we think friendships can never happen for us. We all want it, yet friendship seems to be a rare, special occurrence, and difficult to maintain.

Most of us were much more open to friendship as children. Over the years, we may have learned not to trust so easily, share so much, or love so freely. We may have been betrayed or hurt in some way—perhaps many times. We may have built a wall around ourselves that keeps out the pain—and the friendship.

Children laugh, play, fight, tell secrets, hug, argue, and dance for joy together—all in the space of a few minutes. They hold back nothing, and bounce back instantly. They don't expect perfection or hold on to grudges. They simply enjoy each other and themselves. We can learn a lot from the friendships of children.

I let go of the fears that keep me from friendships.

SUPPORT GROUPS

Whatever we feel, others have felt. Whatever we experience, others have been through before us. Whatever we think, want, need, fear, or wish, other people do too. We can find these people and let them help us. We can discover that we are not so strange, unusual, or unique.

Seeing others who have survived, learned, grown, and changed themselves and their lives can teach us about ourselves and give us hope and a safe, understanding audience.

All we have to do is open ourselves up to the understanding and support available to us from others. Whether we find ourselves in support groups for grief, codependency, overeating, compulsive gambling, alcohol, drug, or sex addictions, we can get help from people who know what we're thinking and feeling—because they've been there.

I can find help in support groups.

EXPECTATIONS

Sometimes we get bogged down with expectations of others they can't possibly fulfill. We may blame them for our problems or believe they are responsible for our health, happiness, and well-being. We may think if only someone else would change, we could too.

But no one is responsible for us but us. Finding someone to blame for our problems won't help us make positive changes *now*. Waiting for someone else to change is like waiting for the sun to rise in the west.

As soon as we let go of our unrealistic expectations, we can discover all the real help other people *can* give us. We can receive love, encouragement, respect, understanding, acceptance, and companionship from others. We can stop waiting to get things from people who just can't give them to us right now, and find others who can.

I let go of my unrealistic expectations of others.

Amends

Other people may sometimes want to make amends to us for their past mistakes. When this happens, we may not feel ready to forgive them or accept their amends. But we can allow others to make amends to us without liking them, approving of their behavior, or letting them become part of our daily lives. If they are able to do something truly positive and helpful for us, it hurts us both if we refuse to let them.

Letting go of our anger long enough to see their sincerity and accept their amends can be the first step toward forgiving others. Forgiveness frees us of the negative emotions of carrying a grudge. It opens space in our minds and hearts for happier thoughts and feelings. By allowing another person to make amends to us, we may also receive the gift of our own forgiveness.

I can accept the amends of others and begin moving toward forgiveness.

JOY

Happiness can be infectious. A truly joyful person can stir up a little joy in everyone around them. But sometimes we may find such a person annoying, exasperating, or even enraging. Their happiness may threaten the wall of cynicism, anger, or self-pity we've constructed around ourselves. This wall may seem self-protective, but may actually keep bad feelings in and good feelings out.

No one else is responsible for our true happiness and peace of mind. But other people can often help us out of a low mood, or offer a fresh, positive viewpoint on a difficult problem or situation. We can begin pulling down the wall between ourselves and others, brick by brick. For a start, we can at least tolerate happy people and gradually grow to feel glad for them. Little by little, we may find ourselves sharing their joy.

I accept, respect, and share in the joy of others.

APPROVAL

Sometimes we seek other people's approval as if our very life depended on it. But approval of our behaviors or choices isn't the same as approval of *us*. We deserve approval simply because we're human.

We may even be suspicious of people who approve of us as we are right now. We may consider others' negative judgments and criticisms of us more appropriate or truthful. But we are not our actions or mistakes.

When we begin to accept and approve of ourselves as we are right now, with all our mistakes and imperfections, we can begin accepting true approval from others. We can stop playing the endless game of approval-seeking for our every action and decision. Instead, we can concentrate on learning, growing, and moving forward from wherever we happen to be.

I approve of myself and accept the approval of others.

Free Lunch

~~~

We are often wary of receiving anything for nothing. We believe we have to pay for everything we get in one way or another. "There's no such thing as a free lunch," may be our guiding motto.

In many cases, this may be sensible. When our egos relate to others without guidance from our higher selves, we give in order to get. When we receive, we fully expect to pay a price.

But our Higher Power offers us many gifts through the highest spiritual selves in others. When we understand giving and receiving from the viewpoint of God and our spirits, we can receive love, help, and abundance with no strings attached. And all the goodness of the universe can flow freely through us.

I accept my Higher Power's infinite generosity and the gifts I can receive through other people.

LAUGHTER

Laughter is a great gift. It can relieve tension, fatigue, boredom, anger, worry, fear, and self-pity. It can help us relate better to others or relax by ourselves.

Often, laughter is indeed the best medicine. When we let go of our negative thoughts and feelings long enough to laugh, we allow ourselves to be healed just a little. When we're stuck on a difficult problem, laughter can free our minds and get our creativity flowing again.

Sometimes laughter sneaks up on us when we expect it least, and perhaps need it most. Sometimes we try to resist it, clinging instead to our negative outlook. Sometimes we have to seek it out, knowing its health-giving power. However it comes to us, we can receive and accept the gift of laughter willingly and gratefully.

I accept the gift of laughter.

STRANGERS

Victor Hugo wrote, "Great perils have this beauty, that they bring to light the fraternity of strangers." In catastrophic circumstances, total strangers suddenly give each other emotional support, first aid, and even save each others' lives. Money, food, clothing, and shelter are shared abundantly.

The love and humanity deep within each of us comes out at these times to remind us that they are *always* there. Whatever walls exist between people are merely creations of our egos. In our daily lives, strangers can give us smiles, inspiration, laughter, kindness. They can bring us products, services, information, and assistance of all kinds.

Everywhere we look, we can see and appreciate the gifts of strangers.

I appreciate all the gifts that come to me through strangers.

LESSONS

We often learn the most from our own mistakes and experiences. But we can also gain understanding and insight into ourselves and our lives by observing others, not to judge them or compete with them, but to gain the benefit of their wisdom and experience. We can often look more clearly and objectively at their situations and behaviors than our own.

Sometimes we learn by teaching—giving advice we need to take ourselves. Sometimes situations in other people's lives, which are similar to our own, reinforce our lessons or choices. Sometimes we can only discover a mistake we've made by seeing someone else do the same thing or make a better choice we didn't think of. We can't all experience everything, but we can learn from each others' experiences, choices, and mistakes.

I can learn from the lessons of other people's lives.

NURTURING RELATIONSHIPS

In some way at some time, we have all been *nurtured* in a relationship, or we wouldn't be alive. The word *nurture* means to nourish, or cause growth and development. We can be nurtured physically, emotionally, mentally, or spiritually.

Nurturing relationships and the people in them aren't perfect. But they can help us develop toward our highest potential in some way. They can help us grow healthier and stronger. They can deepen our knowledge, wisdom, and understanding.

We all need and deserve nurturing relationships with other people. We can have more of these relationships in our lives by recognizing, accepting, and enjoying them.

I now attract and accept healthy, nurturing relationships into my life.

YES

No was one of the first words most of us learned. It may also have been one of the words we heard most often when we were growing up. Sometimes, understanding and accepting *no* was important to our safety. Other times, it may have helped us learn positive, appropriate behavior.

But somewhere along the way, we may also have learned to say no to many good experiences and opportunites. We may have turned down many offers of help, friendship, or love. Saying no may have become almost automatic for us.

We can take the risk of saying yes occasionally. We can begin learning now to say yes to all the good things, feelings, experiences, and opportunities available to us. Gradually, we can learn that it's okay to accept good into our lives. We deserve it.

I can say yes to all the good available in my life.

Setting Boundaries

Learning to receive good also means learning to refuse harm. It means accepting a life free of physical, emotional, mental, and spiritual abuse. Affirming ourselves in this way sometimes means walking away from a conversation, confrontation, or relationship. Sometimes it means asserting ourselves by refusing to do things for others that they can do for themselves.

We are responsible for setting boundaries on what we will accept from others. We can understand and forgive them, but we don't have to accept their abuse.

We deserve to be respected and valued in all our relationships. When we take responsibility for refusing to accept harm, we become freer to accept good.

I accept freedom from harm in all my relationships.

TEACHERS

Ancient wisdom tells us that when the student is ready, the teacher appears. The lessons we need come to us when we're ready to learn them. Often, they come through other people.

The teachers in our lives don't usually instruct us directly, with lectures or coaching. Instead, we learn from our relationships and experiences. Sometimes a teacher appears when we least expect it. We may be worrying about a problem, and suddenly find a book containing exactly the information we need. We may feel we are all alone in the world, and suddenly meet someone who seems to understand us completely.

Our readiness is an important factor in our learning process. Being ready means being open and continuing to take one step at a time, one day at a time.

I accept the teachers and lessons I need into my life.

INTERDEPENDENCE

John Donne wrote, "No man is an island, entire to itself." Humanity is a network of interdependent individuals and groups. We need other people for a wide variety of purposes in our lives. They help us get food, clothing, shelter, electricity, water, transportation, education, and entertainment. They offer us medical care and emotional support. They provide us with companionship and growth experiences.

Each of us, in our own way, contributes these things, and more, to others. As members of the human community, we all deserve to be respected, accepted, valued, and nurtured. We all have roles to play, in both giving and receiving. But we have to take an active role both in recognizing our place in the human community, and in getting what we need from it.

I am an important part of the human community.

SPECIAL RELATIONSHIPS

When we feel especially close to someone, we may want to get them involved in every area of our lives. Sometimes we let our world shrink until it's just us and one other person. When we recognize that our special person can't fulfill all our needs, we may be angry or disappointed. We may try to control them and *make* them give us what we think we need from them.

But all the things we need from others can't come from just one person. No one can ever fulfill all of our needs. We need a variety of relationships in order to receive various kinds of help, support, and growth experiences. Our well-being grows from taking responsibility for ourselves and accepting what we need from others. It means knowing where we can and can't expect to find it.

I let go of expecting too much from my special relationships.

Knowledge

Education doesn't end with our schooling. We continue learning all of our lives. How much we learn is completely up to us. We close ourselves off from learning in many ways. Often, we cling stubbornly to what we already believe is true. This makes learning new, contradictory information impossible. Sometimes we make assumptions or form personal opinions, and call them *knowledge*. Other times we accept what we hear from others, without verifying it in any way.

The world is full of information, ideas, and the perceptions and insights of others. No one can learn everything or keep up with it all. But we can open ourselves up to receiving a little more knowledge every day.

Our minds are as alive as our bodies. We can feed them, exercise them, and help them continue growing in health and fitness all through our lives.

I am open to ever-increasing knowledge.

ABUNDANCE

The positive, loving, spiritual energy of the universe comes to us in many ways. But sometimes we cut ourselves off from some of this energy. We feel guilty or undeserving of all the good available to us. We may believe that scarcity and lack are normal and appropriate. Happiness and abundance may seem selfish or irresponsible to us.

Being greedy, selfish, or irresponsible is not the same as accepting God's abundance. It is merely an expression of insecurity and self-hate. But accepting abundance joyfully is an expression of true love for ourselves, others, and the universe. When we accept the infinite abundance of God's universe, we share it all happily. We know it is here for all of us, and we need never feel deprived.

I accept the flow of God's infinite abundance through my life.

MIRACLES

When wonderful, lucky, miraculous things happen in our lives, how do we react? Do we go around declaring, "I can't believe it?" Do we start looking over our shoulder for a lightning bolt to offset our good fortune?

Life is full of miracles, whether or not we believe in them. When we are open to receiving them joyfully, they flow into our lives freely. When we "can't believe" them, or expect to pay for them with bad luck, they can't do their work in our lives. We dilute their power by not accepting and appreciating them.

We can begin to recognize and accept miracles by simply thinking, "Thank you" over and over, to quiet our doubts and fears. We can replace our old negative reactions with grateful, joyful acceptance of all the miraculous blessings of life.

I joyfully and thankfully accept miracles into my life.

LOVE

Love comes to us through other people in the form of help, companionship, support, encouragement, respect, admiration, forgiveness, nurturing, understanding, and acceptance. It blesses us with peace, contentment, and beauty. Love comes to us as growth, healing, abundance, knowledge, wisdom, and joy. It sneaks up on us with laughter, intuition, and good fortune. It is an affirmation of our existence as spiritual beings.

We can think of all our relationships as expressions of this love. Whether acquaintanceships, friendships, romances, or family kinships, we can think of them all as *love-ships*. We can have loveships with ourselves, our Higher Power, and all of humanity. We can have loveships with nature, animals, and the stars in the sky. We can have a loveship with life.

My relationships with everyone and everything are loveships.

LAKE VISUALIZATION

Now let us imagine a beautiful, sparkling lake. It's fresh, cool, and teeming with life. Fish swim in its depths and, in the twinkling of an eye, burst into the brilliant sunlight and then back into the water. Lush green foliage surrounds the water's edge.

On our left is a river flowing *into* this lake. It's long and winding, bringing a constant supply of clear, clean water from a vast, endless ocean off in the distance. Now we look to the right, where another river flows *out* of the lake. The water rushes happily down this river and back out into the ocean. This constant flow of water, in and out, keeps the lake from becoming stagnant. It keeps the lake *alive*.

We look over and see our name painted on a beautiful sign next to the lake. This is *our* lake. It is *each of us*. The life-giving water flowing through it is the spiritual energy we receive and give.

Spiritual energy flows to me and through me to others.

OUR HIGHER POWER

Introduction

To know that what is impenetrable to us really exists, manifesting itself as the highest wisdom and most radiant beauty . . . this knowledge, this feeling, is at the center of true religiousness.

—Albert Einstein

However we choose to understand and envision our Higher Power or God is up to each of us. Our spirituality is a personal, private aspect of ourselves. Our relationship with our Higher Power can be the most intimate of all our relationships.

The "true religiousness" Einstein talks about has nothing to do with churches. It has to do with a point of view that accepts *something* greater than ourselves at work in the universe and in our own lives. This Power is completely positive—loving, accepting, forgiving, expansive, and inclusive. It manifests itself in everything good. It just keeps endlessly building, creating, healing, and renewing.

Our Higher Power is our source of spiritual energy, offering an infinite supply of everything we need for our well-being. It allows us to express goodness, each in our own way. But to receive this energy and express it, we need to recognize and open ourselves to it. We need to take the time to let go of our fears and doubts.

We don't have to believe any kind of dogma or doctrine. All we have to do is open our minds just a little to the possibility of a Higher Power capable and willing to help us in every way. We can start by *acting as if* this Power exists. We can let ourselves experience our Higher Power.

If we already have faith and an understanding of our Higher Power, we can help this faith grow and deepen. We can remind ourselves daily to let our Higher Power fill us with loving, healing, creative spiritual energy. Then we'll be able to spread it throughout our lives and the world.

Our Deep Self

How can we reach a Higher Power, a source of perfect knowledge, understanding, and spirituality? How can we tap into this infinite well of love and wisdom for the answers we seek?

Thomas Merton wrote, "It is by the door of the deep self that we enter into the spiritual knowledge of God." But we can only find our "deep self" by reaching beyond all our other selves that cover it up.

Our ego may distract us from our inward search in many ways—with fears, doubts, worries, delusions, and rationalizations. These voices in our minds can be very loud and persistent.

But our spirit, our "deep self," waits calmly and patiently for us to discover it. And when we do, in quiet meditation, we are ready to receive the knowledge and experience of our Higher Power.

I look for my Higher Power deep within myself.

MEDITATION

Meditation is a way to relax our bodies and quiet our minds. It gives us a break from all the busy activity of our daily lives. It helps us maintain an open channel of communication with our Higher Power.

We sit comfortably in a quiet place, close our eyes, and breathe slowly and deeply. We let our muscles relax. We may count down slowly from ten to one or focus our attention on our breathing. This helps us turn away from the distractions around and within us.

When we are in a deeply relaxed state, we simply open ourselves to our Higher Power's presence. We can ask questions or repeat affirmations. When we feel ready, we can take a deep breath, perhaps count back up from one to ten, and return to our normal consciousness, feeling relaxed, peaceful, and serene.

I use meditation as a tool for opening up to my Higher Power.

Our Spiritual Source

The energy that brings electrical power into our homes comes from the electric company. It is generated at a central location and sent out through cables to wherever it is needed—provided we pay the bill.

The spiritual energy within us comes from our Higher Power. An infinite supply of love, peace, joy, forgiveness, hope, and wisdom flows from this source. It's always available, to anyone, anywhere, by simply recognizing and accepting it. And it's absolutely free!

Unlike the electric company, our Higher Power does not require cables or wires to transmit spiritual energy. We don't even have to go to a church or any special place to get it. We are already linked to the Power source. All we have to do is reach deep inside ourselves to find our connection to our Higher Power.

My Higher Power is the source of all my spiritual energy.

DESCRIBING THE ELEPHANT

There is an old story about people trying to describe an elephant by feeling it in the dark. Everyone described it differently, depending on whether they happened to be feeling its trunk, leg, ear, or ivory tusk.

We are like those people. When we try to define God or our Higher Power, we each arrive at a description based on our own experiences and perceptions. Consequently, we have a vast array of differing concepts.

No one describing the elephant was *wrong*—they just didn't have the whole picture. It seems we humans are also in the dark when it comes to "seeing" God. But we don't have to throw out the idea of a Higher Power just because our knowledge is incomplete. We can accept the limits of our understanding, and tolerate other people's perceptions, even if they are very different from ours.

I accept my limited understanding, and focus on a simple concept of a loving Higher Power.

THE POWER OF LOVE

Many people believe that God is the essence of love. The power of love is indeed greater than any other we know of. Its mere presence can transform any situation or relationship.

We see the power of love whenever we help or are helped, whenever we forgive or are forgiven. Wherever there is hope, faith, peace, or wisdom, there is love. Love has the power to create, heal, and transform. When we feel it, we need nothing else. When we don't, nothing else satisfies.

But we don't need to wait for special relationships with other people to feel love. It is always available to us, deep within ourselves as our spiritual essence, our innermost core, our connection to our Higher Power. It is quietly waiting for us to recognize it. We can find it by simply accepting it into our consciousness.

I am filled with the power of love.

In God's Image

Many of us were taught that humankind was created in God's image and likeness. So we looked at ourselves and decided that what we saw must also be in God. We formed a concept of a Higher Power that has our emotions, imperfections, and even physical characteristics. We may have been thinking of God in our image rather than ourselves in God's image.

We were also taught that God is everywhere and knows all. Since we know our bodies and minds can't do that, then God must be spirit, not body. If we were created in His image, perhaps we are not just bodies, egos, emotions, and minds. Perhaps we too are spirits and *that* is the part of us created in God's image. Perhaps somewhere deep inside us, there is a spark of God's infinite capacity for love, forgiveness, peace, joy, and creativity.

I let go of human restrictions on my image of God.

LIGHT VISUALIZATION

Imagine yourself on a deserted beach. This is one of the most beautiful places you've ever seen. The sky is blue, and the sun warms your body as you stand at the edge of the water. You are relaxed, peaceful, and completely safe.

Now imagine a ray of sunshine gently flowing into the top of your head and through your entire body. You are filled with a beautiful golden light that heals and strengthens you in every way. You are filled with only love, peace, happiness, health, joy, understanding, and forgiveness.

Stretch out your arms in front of you and feel the light flowing out over the water and into the world. The supply is infinite; the light and love of your Higher Power remains within you and flows through you.

The light and love of my Higher Power flows in me and through me.

"Came to Believe . . ."

It's important to take the time we need to develop our own individual concept of God or our Higher Power. It doesn't happen overnight. It happens gradually, as our experiences and insights build upon each other.

Our faith and understanding is like a budding flower: growing slowly, opening more and more as it drinks in the nourishment of the soil, air, and water. There is no hurry. Each phase of the blossoming is beautiful in its own way and is necessary in preparation for the next.

We can accept the blossoming of our faith just as we accept the blossoming of the flower. It doesn't matter how many years we've been alive. It doesn't matter how far along we think our friends and neighbors are. All that matters is that we keep seeking nourishing experiences that will help our faith bloom.

I accept my own natural pace of spiritual development.

OUR GOD IMAGE

The many different words and images we use to talk about God or Our Higher Power reflect our confusion.

As children, we may have been presented with an image of an old man on a throne or in a cloud in the sky. Someone told us about God in a way they thought we could understand. Or maybe it was the only way *they* could understand. We can now examine our childhood image of God and decide how we feel about it. We no longer have to accept it as our own.

We can visualize our Higher Power any way we wish. We can imagine a man, woman, or child. We can think of a bright light or electric energy pulsing through the universe. These images are only symbols, and we can choose whatever symbol represents for us a loving, healing source of spirituality.

I can choose my own image of my Higher Power.

FEAR OF GOD

Fear of the dark is common in children. We felt threatened by what we couldn't see and recognize as harmless. Even as adults, we may feel uncomfortable in the dark or in unfamiliar surroundings. How much more frightening might be some vague concept of a powerful being that has never been satisfactorily explained, either to our senses or our minds?

But we can release our fear of God, even if we don't really understand what God is. We can fill our minds with images of a loving, healing, helpful entity. We can choose to believe in a Power of infinite peace and joy. In choosing faith, hope, love, and acceptance of our limited understanding, we choose freedom from fear.

I choose to release my fears and see only a loving, healing, and forgiving God.

PRAYER

~⚬~

Prayer does not necessarily mean reciting special words, or thanking our Higher Power for the help we receive, or listing our requests. It can be all of these things, some, or none of them.

Prayer is any thought directed toward communication with our Higher Power and an awareness of our spirituality. It can be as simple as appreciating a warm sunny day or a nourishing, cleansing rain shower. It can be as complex as pondering the meaning of life and the purpose of humanity.

Since our connection to our Higher Power lies not in any building or book or set of words, we can experience this connection anywhere, anytime. We always carry within us our connection to our Higher Power and our own spirituality. Prayer is simply taking a moment to become aware of it.

Prayer is a natural part of my day.

Spiritual Awakening

We may feel confused by the idea of a *spiritual awakening*. We may think we aren't making any progress on our spiritual path because we don't feel completely "awakened" to our spirituality.

But for most of us, our spiritual awakening is very gradual. It's like a slow, natural awakening from a long deep sleep. We yawn, stretch, blink, moan, and slip back into our dreams. We linger at the edge of consciousness for as long as we can.

We shouldn't judge ourselves or become impatient. It's a natural, appropriate, and necessary process. Our Higher Power and our inner spiritual selves do not rouse us with a sudden, shocking alarm. They whisper to us softly, and lead us gently and slowly to spiritual consciousness. All we have to do is allow it to happen.

I allow my Higher Power to guide me to an awareness of my deepest spiritual self.

FAITH

~~~⁂~~~

We may think that faith is something special that only very religious people have. But the truth is that we are always placing our faith *somewhere*. In the past, we may have put our faith in alcohol or other drugs, food, or a particular person or relationship. We may have believed that one day, some event or relationship would come into our lives and magically transform them. Invariably, we have been disappointed.

The trouble was in placing our faith outside of ourselves. We have learned that we can't trust our egos to guide us to love and happiness. But we are not just our egos. There is another, deeper part of ourselves that is indeed worthy of our trust and faith. It is the part that knows only our highest and best. It is our connection to our Higher Power and the highest spiritual selves in other people. It is our spirit.

I place my faith in my Higher Power, my own spirit, and that of others.

OPEN-MINDEDNESS

Faith has been defined as "belief which is not based on proof." It may be difficult to let go of our attachment to the idea of scientific method and proof. But we should remember that even scientists must be open-minded. How else could they ever make new discoveries? How else could human knowledge keep evolving and expanding.

We can now prove the existence of radio frequencies and micro-organisms. But before invention of sophisticated instruments to detect them, they still existed. Isn't it possible, then, that God and spiritual energy exist even if we can't prove them scientifically? An open mind is an open door through which our own truths can emerge.

I let go of my attachment to old ideas, and become open to new truths.

Act As If

~∞~

If we have trouble accepting the concept of God or a Higher Power, we can try for just one day, acting as if we do believe. We can imagine that this Power is all-knowing, all-loving, and always available with perfect guidance. We can act as if this Power has only our well-being and best interests at heart.

We can try to reach this Power in prayer and meditation, praying only for the knowledge of what is best in every situation and the ability to carry that out. When we relax our bodies and open our minds to whatever this Higher Power wishes to convey, we can notice what happens to our outlook and behavior.

The little bit of fear and doubt we have given up today by acting as if can be released again and again. Gradually, we will grow in trust, love, and knowledge of a Higher Power.

Today I will think and behave as if I completely trust in a Power greater than myself.

INNER GUIDANCE

When we quiet the noise of our conscious minds—our superficial egos—another, softer voice can be heard. This voice offers help, guidance, and support. It tells us, quite simply and clearly, our Higher Power's will for us and how we may accomplish it.

This Inner Guidance will never lead us to any thought or action that is destructive to ourselves or others. That is one way we can be sure which of the voices in our minds we are hearing. Our Inner Guidance will not harm or deceive us.

We can ask this Inner Guidance questions about our lives and what we should do. If we relax and trust, letting go of fears and doubts, answers will come to us as ideas or through books, other people, or in some other way.

In stillness, I hear the voice of my Inner Guidance.

INFLOWING

We may joyfully accept positive, loving, spiritual energy when we perceive it as coming from our Higher Power. But when it comes to us from other people, we may not quite trust it. When we feel this way, we have forgotten that our Higher Power often sends us energy *through* other people. The love, guidance, assistance, and wisdom we receive from others really comes from our Higher Power.

The positive energy of our Higher Power can circulate freely throughout the world only if we let it. This means sending out as many peaceful, joyful, and loving thoughts and actions as we can. But it also means *receiving* the same kind of positive energy from others. When we allow ourselves to channel good thoughts, feelings, and actions, inflowing is as important as outflowing.

I joyfully accept the good coming to me through other people.

SURRENDER

To our egos, surrender implies giving up, admitting defeat, *losing*. But to our spirits, surrender to a Higher Power can mean freedom and joy.

When we surrender to feelings of romantic love, we become emotionally vulnerable. Our feelings for another person may not be returned. We may love our children and feel hurt by their adolescent rebellion or adult choices. Sometimes people we love die or move away. But only by taking the risk of surrender can we ever hope to experience the joy of love.

Surrender to our Highest Power may feel risky, but it is actually the only relationship guaranteed not to hurt us. It can only enhance, expand, and develop the love within our highest selves.

I surrender to a Higher Power that only loves, helps, and protects me.

KEEP IT SIMPLE

The various philosophies and doctrines of religions are anything but simple. The concepts of religion may seem lofty and confusing, some of the rules arbitrary and pointless. This may be a reason many of us turn away from religion or even the idea of a Higher Power.

Our concept of our Higher Power must be *simple*. Otherwise, we may get bogged down in intellectual debates and give up on trying to discover our own spirituality.

We can Keep It Simple by letting go of our fears, worries, and confusion. We can focus on the thought that we have a spiritual aspect, a little part of us that always sees and acts in our best interests—if we let it. We can believe that a Power greater than us is always available to help us—or just act as if we do.

I keep my thoughts about my Higher Power and spirituality clear and simple.

ACCEPTING GOD'S LOVE

One reason we may sometimes have difficulty accepting an all-loving Higher Power is that we feel basically unlovable. Perhaps we can't imagine being accepted and loved so completely.

The metaphor often used in describing God's love for us is the father-child relationship. Consequently, our relationship with our human father can have an important effect on our beliefs about a Higher Power. Since human fathers are imperfect, our relationships with them might have been difficult or painful.

But we don't have to let this cut us off from the infinite and unconditional love of our Higher Power. We can accept that this love may have no human equivalent, at least not in our experience. We can decide there's a first time for everything, and open ourselves to accepting God's perfect love.

I accept God's love, understanding, forgiveness, and help.

MAGICAL THINKING

Believing in a relationship with our Higher Power isn't the same as magical thinking. We don't turn our lives and wills over to our Higher Power and then expect to live happily ever after. We still have free will and choices to make.

Magical thinking is believing we can control situations, circumstances, and other people. It often means pinning our hopes for happiness and well-being on some future event, circumstance, or relationship.

Accepting a Higher Power is the opposite of magical thinking. It is accepting what we can't control, and taking responsibility for our choices. This can bring wonderful events, circumstances, and relationships into our lives. But we must do the work of getting, and staying, out of God's way.

I accept my responsibility in my relationship with my Higher Power.

THE BALLOON

We can picture all the worries, problems, situations, and relationships we want to turn over to our Higher Power, give each one a name, and imagine writing it on a piece of paper. As we place all the pieces of paper into a basket tied to a big, bright balloon, we visualize letting the balloon carry the basket up into the sky. As we watch it drift away, we know that our Higher Power will receive it and take care of it all.

Now we notice another balloon, off in the distance, drifting gently toward us. It is our favorite color and carries a basket containing everything we truly want— health, happiness, love, serenity, joy, forgiveness, courage, and wisdom. It continues drifting slowly toward us until it lands gently. We reach into the basket and accept the gifts our Higher Power has sent.

I turn over everything in my life to my Higher Power, and gratefully accept my Higher Power's gifts.

TURN IT OVER

⚜

Turning over our will and lives to a Power greater than ourselves does not mean that we never again have to face our problems. It means accepting the things we can't control, and getting help with those we can.

Turning it over doesn't mean becoming a slave; it means transcending our own ego. Our Higher Power doesn't want to enslave or control us, but respects our free will while offering an inexhaustible supply of unerring assistance and guidance. When we use our free will to accept this help, there is nothing we can't handle.

We turn over our will and lives to our Higher Power one step at a time, one day at a time. When we have a difficult problem, we can turn it over. When a dark cloud doesn't seem to have a silver lining, we can turn it over and we'll find one.

I turn over my will and life to a Power greater than my ego.

Spiritual Growth

~∞~

Our relationship with our Higher Power, like all living things, grows and changes. Through experience, we learn more and more about our Higher Power's infinite love. At various times, we feel patience, understanding, forgiveness, encouragement, comfort, and joy coming to us from our Higher Power. As we grow older, we may discover new lessons for us in our changing bodies, long-term relationships, and the constant flow of endings and beginnings.

We may question our Higher Power when life seems difficult or prayers seem to go unanswered. But these can be times of growth too. Sometimes we try so hard to understand, finally realize that we can't, and give up. Often, this is the time our Higher Power floods our consciousness with profound insight.

I allow my relationship with my Higher Power to grow and change.

Our Free Will

~~~

Our Higher Power never tries to control our free will, but respects it as our gift and our right. God won't ever force us to do or believe anything.

But our Higher Power also won't wave a magic wand and make us and the world perfect. God creates, builds, and extends in infinite love; forgives, understands, and accepts us unconditionally; helps, nurtures, and facilitates our growth. But God won't rescue us from our own free will. We have to make our own choices.

Whether we choose love or hate, fear or trust, anger or forgiveness, misery or joy, is completely up to us. We make the choices ourselves, consciously or unconsciously, every moment of every day. When we choose to align our free will with our Higher Power's will for us, we discover true peace and happiness.

I use my free will to choose love, trust, forgiveness, and joy.

POWER

~~~~~

There are no less than sixteen definitions of the word *power* in a typical English dictionary. The one definition that springs to our minds first can have a tremendous impact on our concept of a Higher Power. If we are used to thinking of *power* as authority or domination over others, then we may fear accepting a Higher Power. We may perceive any Power greater than ourselves as threatening.

Our Higher Power doesn't want to dominate or control us. Only egos think that way. Our Higher Power's energy, ability, and wisdom exist to help us transcend our own. We can choose to define *power* in a positive way. We can accept an *energy* or *ability* greater than that of our bodies, egos, and personalities: an infinite loving *wisdom*, capable of giving us all the help we will ever need.

I trust in an Energy, Ability, and Wisdom greater than myself.

SCIENCE AND SPIRITUALITY

Scientists have discovered a world of tiny, energetic particles within the physical forms we see. At its most basic level, everything can be seen as pure energy. We can think of this energy as the energy of our Higher Power or God. Whatever we call it, the energy controlling the universe can be seen as positive, creative, and consistent. It seems to be able to control the universe in an orderly fashion through the laws of physics and mathematics. Even though we don't fully understand it, we know it exists.

Learning more about science may bring us closer to understanding our spiritual natures. Someday, we may clearly understand the energy within us that always leans toward love, peace, healing, and creativity. But until then, we can simply accept and enjoy its presence.

I accept both science and spirituality as gifts from my Higher Power.

A Path with a Heart

For many people, religion and membership in a congregation can provide great comfort, support, and spiritual nourishment. But for others, religion may only mean harsh dogma or pious self-righteousness. A religious community may seem more social or political than spiritual.

In Carlos Castaneda's *Journey to Ixtlan*, Don Juan counsels, "Choose a path with a heart." Our previous experience with a religious organization may not have felt gentle, loving, accepting, and spiritual, but that doesn't mean we can never find one that is this way. Finding "a path with a heart" may take some exploring.

We don't have to stick with our family's religion or church. We may even find our path outside of any church or religion. With the help and guidance of our Higher Power, we can find our path in our own way.

A spiritual path is one of love, peace, joy, and forgiveness.

RECEIVING GOD'S GIFTS

If we turn to our Higher Power with all kinds of assumptions and expectations, we may be disappointed. Our Higher Power may not answer our prayers in the ways we anticipate. Whatever we think we need or want may not be what God knows is best for us.

Mother Teresa has said, "Even God cannot fill what is full." If our mind is full of the voices of our ego and our old negative tapes, we can't hear God's voice. If our heart is full of fear, worry, and old rigid beliefs, we can't accept love, peace, and new truths.

But if we let go of our grasping, clutching hold on familiar beliefs and expectations, we make room in our lives for God. If we let go of our attachment to all things, circumstances, and relationships we think will make us happy, we make room for true happiness.

I let go of my old beliefs and make room for God's gifts.

GRATITUDE

Thankfulness is one of the most powerful ways we can communicate with God. Everywhere we look, all day long, there are things to be grateful for. We can even thank God for things we usually complain about, things that feel more like burdens than blessings. We can thank God for *everything*.

Gratitude is a decision we make to see everything in a new way. Even if we start out thinking we have little or nothing to be grateful for, eventually we're able to see more and more.

We can stop for a moment, right now, and say "Thank you" to our Higher Power. We can be grateful for *everything* we see, hear, think, feel, know, and imagine. We can just be grateful.

Thank you, God.

SERENITY

INTRODUCTION

I am a little world made cunningly of elements, and an angelic sprite.

—John Donne

Imagine a situation where you were unaware of one of the aspects of yourself as a person—the physical, emotional, or intellectual part of you. You had it, but you didn't *know* you had it, and so you acted as if you *didn't* have it. You'd be severely handicapped in everything you tried to do.

That's how many of us are about our spirituality—our "angelic sprite." We don't *know* we have it, so we act as if we don't have it. This hampers our every effort. It's like trying to work out a puzzle using only our hands and not our intellect, or trying to conduct a personal relationship using only our rational, logical minds and none of our emotions.

Spirituality is part of each of us, whether or not we know it. If we do know it, and allow ourselves to experience our spirituality more fully, it can enhance every area of our lives. It can help us pull together all our faculties—physical, emotional, intellectual, and spiritual—and use them harmoniously for our highest well-being.

The result of this harmony is *serenity*. We waken the "angelic sprite" sleeping within us, and let it guide our thoughts, feelings, and behavior. It fills us with deep acceptance and understanding. It frees us from our fears, doubts, and worries. It shows us the love, peace, and joy that were there all along, deep inside us.

105

SPIRITUAL ENERGY

We often think of energy as the ability to move our bodies. But human beings also have emotional, mental, and spiritual energies. Each of these requires exercise, nourishment, and rest.

We care for our bodies with food, water, sleep, and physical activity. We nourish our minds by thinking, reading, working puzzles, learning new facts, and relaxing. We care for ourselves emotionally by respecting our feelings, understanding and expressing them, and growing in our relationships.

We receive spiritual nourishment from our Higher Power. We can provide our spiritual selves with rest in meditation. We can exercise our spirituality by sending loving thoughts and actions into the world. Our awareness of our spiritual energy helps it flow freely from our Higher Power to us, and through us to others.

I am an open channel of spiritual energy.

GROWING SYTLES

Unique learning styles are not limited to students in school. We all continue to learn and grow throughout our lives. Some of us find help with our growth through reading informative and inspirational literature, while others prefer lectures or tapes. Some of us grow most through our contacts with other people. Others find that daily prayer and meditation produce the most profound changes in their lives.

We can try all the help available to us on our spiritual path, and then concentrate on those sources and methods that work best for us. We can find and use our own unique way to learn and grow spiritually. The only right way is the way that works for us.

My own style of learning and growing will lead me on my spiritual path.

An Attitude of Prayer

Like so many other ideas we learned in childhood, our beliefs about prayer may no longer serve us. But we are free to let the old ideas go and find new ways of thinking and praying that are better for us now.

Prayer need not be done in special places, times, or ways. We can develop an *attitude* of prayer that never leaves us. We have an attitude of prayer when we are open to the love, beauty, joy, and peace available to us all; when we see mountains and sunsets with joy and awe; when we look at the smallest grain of sand on the beach or star in the sky with wonder and gratitude.

We become living prayers when we make the effort needed to really listen to others, when we care for a living thing, when we apologize for our errors, or offer help where it's needed.

Every thought and action can be a prayer.

PAIN

Kahlil Gibran wrote, ". . . could you keep your heart in wonder at the daily miracles of your life, your pain would not seem less wondrous than your joy." That we humans can feel pain is indeed as wondrous as the fact that we can feel joy, because the lessons we learn from our pain can be transformational and miraculous.

Pain is often a signal that we need to make some changes. We can listen to the messages within our pain and grow closer to our spiritual selves. We can let our spirits use our bodies to tell us what to do—and *not* do.

Keeping our hearts and minds focused on the daily miracles of life enables us to learn all our lessons, hear all our messages, and grow in love, peace, and spirituality. Each experience—joyful or painful—is a necessary and wondrous step on our journey.

I am open to all the lessons within my painful experiences.

QUIET TIME

~~~~~~~

Our lives may be busy or hectic. Our days may seem full of other people's needs and demands on us. But we can always find a few minutes to be quietly alone with ourselves.

This time is important because it helps us maintain balance between our outer and inner worlds. It gives us a chance to remember our true beliefs, goals, and spirituality. It revives and refreshes us for the work we need to do.

We can spend this time with our eyes closed, relaxing our bodies, and breathing deeply and slowly. Or we can just focus on watching the sun setting or listening to birds singing. We can empty our minds of worry about the past and future, concentrating only on the present moment.

Our Quiet Time is just for us. We need and deserve it, and it's up to us to take it.

I take a few minutes every day to be quiet with myself.

ACCEPTANCE

Many of us have learned to judge everything. We may label every action, attitude, belief, event, choice, and person as right or wrong, good or bad.

Making such judgments may have become automatic for us. When someone tells us of a decision they've made, we may instantly tell them whether we think they are right or wrong. When we see or hear about a situation or relationship, we may quickly choose which side to defend and begin attacking the other.

But we don't have to judge everything that comes into our awareness. When we let go of these constant judgments, we begin to see everything differently. We begin learning to accept the things we can't control. We stop wasting our time and energy trying to decree how the whole world should be. We find the peacefulness, joy, and contentment of true acceptance.

I let go of my judgments, and accept everything with serenity.

INNER PRAYER

Common wisdom tells us to be careful of what we pray for, because we might get it. If we think of our deepest beliefs and expectations or our vivid thoughts and fantasies as prayers, the wisdom of this advice is clear.

If we believe in scarcity and lack, how will we ever find abundance and prosperity? If we frequently imagine conflict, how likely are we to know harmony and peace? If we truly expect failure, how can success find us?

Our deepest beliefs, attitudes, and expectations find their way into reality. Whatever we really think of ourselves, other people, and life tends to come true for us. By letting go of old programming, we can start "praying" for what we truly want. When we stop thinking of fears and doubts, they begin to lose their power. When we stop believing good things are impossible, anything becomes possible.

I release all my negative beliefs and expectations.

POINT OF VIEW

❧

If you hear a knock at your door and you're expecting a friend, you may feel glad. But your reaction to a knock at the door might be very different if you're expecting someone who is quite late; if you're not expecting anyone; if you're busy and don't want to be disturbed; or if you're alone on a dark, stormy night. Your experiences of the knock depend on your point of view.

The more different points of view we can see in any situation, the greater our understanding and serenity. We can let go of clinging stubbornly to one perspective. We can accept that it is only our *perception* of any experience that determines our response. There is always another way of looking at anything. The broader our perspective, the more serene our response will be.

There is always another way of looking at everything.

LEVELS OF SELF

We can think of ourselves as a set of ascending steps. On the lowest step, we have our physical step. We experience the physical world with our physical senses. We follow our strong desires for food and protection from disease and injury to keep our bodies alive.

On the next step is our emotional self. Here we may experience feelings that aren't directly related to our physical self and aren't necessarily rational or logical. Feelings of romantic love, anger, sadness, and many of our fears are on this level.

The third step is our rational, logical, intellectual self—the level of reason.

The highest step is our spirituality. This level is perfect peace and universal, unconditional love. It connects us to our Higher Power and the spirit of other people. It transcends the other three, but uses them to help us learn, grow, and evolve spiritually.

All the levels of my true self thrive in harmony.

SPIRITUAL ICE CREAM

~~~~~

When we haven't yet allowed ourselves to experience our spirituality, we often confuse it with emotionalism. This is because we use words like "love" to talk about spirituality. But words and experience aren't the same thing.

For someone who hasn't experienced ice cream, the words *ice cream* have no meaning. But that doesn't mean ice cream doesn't exist, or that millions of people don't enjoy it all the time. Spirituality, like ice cream, has to be experienced firsthand to be understood and enjoyed.

Reading about ice cream won't give us the experience of it. Likewise, reading about spirituality won't help us unless it leads us to discover spirituality for ourselves. What we're looking for, what we really need and want isn't in the words. It's in ourselves.

I look for my spirituality deep inside myself.

TOOLS

Someday we may be able to maintain our inner peace and serenity all the time, under any circumstances. But until then, we can use many tools to help us experience the tranquility and contentment we seek.

We can surround ourselves with cleanliness, order, and beauty. We can unclutter our environment to help unclutter our thoughts. We can turn off the TV, radio, or other noise, and learn to enjoy our own company or to focus fully and quietly on others.

We can read books, listen to tapes, and watch movies that are uplifting and inspiring. We can record our thoughts, feelings, and prayers in a journal. We can write, speak, sing, or think affirmations. We can practice meditation and visualization in our own special ways, times, and places. We can use whatever works for us.

I use all the tools available to help me find inner peace.

Letting Go

Sometimes the best way we can help ourselves is by letting go of some familiar pattern of thinking or behaving. But we may resist and blame our difficulties on another person or circumstance.

We may attach ourselves to unhappy or unhealthy situations and relationships with anger, fear, or worry. We may cling relentlessly to our expectations, point of view, or desire for control. These vines of attachment may grow wild and take over our lives, keeping us stuck in misery and pain.

But we can let go of the obstacles to our happiness and well-being when we recognize that their roots are within us. We can weed out the vines and choose love, peace, joy, and forgiveness.

I let go of all attachments standing in the way of my well-being.

INNER PEACE

We can discover freedom from tumultuous emotions and negative thoughts. We can learn that peace orginates *inside*, not outside, of us.

When we let go of our delusion that something will someday make us happy, we can concentrate on the peace and contentment of the present moment. Inner peace is always found in the here and now. It waits quietly for us to discover it.

We can turn our conscious minds away from worries, fears, regrets, expectations, and the busyness of our daily lives. Then all the love, beauty, joy, and peacefulness of our deep spiritual selves can come through to our awareness.

I allow my deep inner peace to fill my conscious mind.

SPIRITUAL SELF-CARE

Our heart beats continuously without our thinking about it. Likewise, whether or not we've become aware of our spirits, they are alive within us.

We can learn about our hearts and help them function best by giving them proper rest, exercise, and nutrition. We can care also for our spiritual selves by filling our thoughts with positive, uplifting ideas. We can read inspirational literature, and pray and meditate regularly. We can avoid negative and harmful situations and people. We can get our egos out of the way, and let our spirits guide, help, and heal us.

Just like our hearts, our spirits are always alive. But with a little effort, we can help them help us.

I care for my spiritual self in every way I can.

OUR DAILY LIVES

Anyone who has suffered from "jet lag" knows the value of consistency in our daily schedules. Sleeping for the same length of time, at about the same time each night is beneficial to our bodies and minds. Eating nutritious foods at regular intervals keeps us healthy and energetic. Meditating, spending quiet time alone, reading, praying, exercising, and spending time with others on a regular daily schedule has the best results.

Frequently changing our routines keeps us in a constant state of imbalance. Instead of focusing on the here and now, we're always recovering from our latest schedule change.

Regular routines needn't be boring or rigid. They keep our bodies fit and our minds alert. They help us do everything better—including finding and maintaining our spirituality.

I order my daily life in a balanced, consistent way.

BELIEF

~∞~

If we are treated by a doctor we don't like, in whom we have no confidence, our bodies may not respond well to the treatment. But if we have great faith in our doctor, our response may be even better than the treatment alone would indicate. What we truly believe affects everything in our lives.

One way to minimize and release our negative beliefs is to concentrate on our positive ones. In meditation, we can focus on our most reassuring thoughts about our Higher Power. We can keep our minds full of confidence, hope, and trust by regularly reading inspirational literature and spending time with positive, healthy people.

We can use our beliefs to help heal our bodies and our lives. Recognizing the power of our beliefs is the beginning.

I focus on my highest, most positive beliefs.

OUR SPIRITUAL CUPBOARD

When our cupboards are nearly bare, we often find ourselves drawn to them—searching shelf after shelf for what isn't there. Filled with an insatiable hunger, we may eat everything we can find, but nothing satisfies. When our cupboards are full, we may look through them occasionally, but actually eat less. Just knowing there is plenty available whenever we want it is enough.

We may have spent many years searching for happiness, comfort, love, God, or spirituality. We may have searched the shelves, sampling every religion or philosophy, and still felt unsatisfied. Everything we found only left us hungrier than before.

When we finally give up searching outside ourselves, we begin looking inward. We find that our own spiritual cupboards are never bare. And at last we rest, content in the knowledge that we are already full.

Inside me is an infinite supply of spiritual energy.

Our Self-Image

What we think of ourselves often comes from what others have told us and how they have treated us. Most of us were never told how truly wonderful we are.

We may think of ourselves as the sum total of our mistakes, or as merely our bodies, egos, and personalities. But we are much more than that. Deep within each of us lives another kind of being—a being of perfect love, peace, beauty, harmony, and joy.

No matter how many layers of fear and doubt cover it up, we can always find this living spirit within us. We can let go of all the false images we've had of ourselves. We can remember our true identity.

When we recognize this deep inner self, we can begin using our outer self to follow its wisdom and express its love. It is who we truly are.

I am a wise, loving, spiritual being.

HAPPINESS

We may pray for specific things or events that we believe will make us happy. We may visualize them frequently and in great detail. We may work hard to make them come into reality just the way we want. But when they do, we may wonder why we still aren't happy or our happiness seems so brief and hollow.

The Eleventh Step of the Twelve Step program advises us to meditate and pray only for the knowledge of God's will and the power to carry it out. This doesn't mean we don't deserve or can't have happiness; it means we don't always know what will truly make us happy. None of the objects, situations, events, or relationships we wish for can create the real, complete, and permanent happiness that is God's will for us.

I pray for and visualize only my perfect happiness and well-being, and I let God choose how I'll get it.

Our Own Path

Each of us is on a unique spiritual path. We try to listen to our Higher Power and our inner truth, and let these guide our actions. We learn the lessons we need to learn through our experiences.

No one else's path is ever quite the same as ours. We have enough to handle on our own path, without trying to interfere with anyone else's. We can let others follow their path, listen to their Higher Power and inner truth, and learn their own lessons.

Likewise, we can take care not to let others interfere with our path. We can avoid other people's negativity, judgments, and doubts. We can stop looking for their approval, and instead trust God and ourselves. We can stop arguing, defending, and explaining ourselves. We can strengthen our faith in God and ourselves by sticking to our own path.

Guided by my Higher Power, I travel my own spiritual path.

INSIGHT

When we overlook the obvious, we can often gain *in-sight* into the real nature of a conflict or problem. For example, if we hold off on responding to someone's anger, we can look deeper and see what's really behind it. Fear, guilt, or low self-worth often send out anger as a defense.

We don't try to see beyond the surface so we can judge others. We do it to gain a deeper understanding of all the situations and people in our lives. The more we understand, the more we can respond with love.

Sometimes insight seems to come to us out of nowhere. Sometimes we have to work at seeing beyond the surface. But true insight always comes from the deep inner self that connects us to our Higher Power. It's a gift we only have to be willing to receive.

I accept the loving insight my Higher Power offers to me.

OPTIMISM

We often view a negative attitude as *realistic*, or even *mature*. We may believe it protects us somehow—we can't be disappointed if we always expect the worst.

On the other hand, we often see optimism as naive, *un*realistic, and even irresponsible. We use the label "Pollyanna" to ridicule optimistic people. But we forget the real story of Pollyanna: She never let life's troubles dampen her joyful outlook. She wasn't blind to all the tragic and bothersome things that happened, but she also saw all the wonderful things, and let go of wasted worry and self-pity.

Pollyanna's unflappable optimism annoyed many of the jaded adults in her life. But they soon realized that optimism made Pollyanna happy, while pessimism only made them unhappy. Happiness is our choice.

I desire and expect only good to come to me, and I believe it will.

Spiritual Centering

Our center is the root of everything in our lives. Some of us think we are centered in our religion, family, or ethnic heritage. Some of us think of our career or our favorite hobby as our center. Some of us keep pulling up our root and trying out new centers.

All these things we normally think of as our center are really outside of us. Deep within us is our true center—our spiritual core. When we recognize our spirit as our center, all the areas of our lives—religion, family, ethnicity, careers, and hobbies— can grow as stong, healthy brances of ourselves.

With spirituality as our center, we can weather the storms of life with serenity. We can face challenges with courage. We can make choices wisely. Our Higher Power's love can flow into our spiritual root and through all our branches, nourishing our lives.

I am centered in my deep, inner self.

SELFISHNESS

Some of us may feel guilty for spending time and attention on our spiritual growth and development. We may have old tapes in our minds, suggesting we "get outside ourselves" or "put others first."

This may be good advice in many instances. But many of us have more trouble getting *inside* ourselves. We may *always* put others first, or put our ego-self first, ignoring our true self.

Much of this confusion may lie in our misunderstanding the word "self." Focusing attention on our ego-self may lead us to disregard others. But learning to focus on our deep, inner, spiritual self—our *true* self—manifests in a serenity that blesses everyone in our lives.

Turning inward to find our spirituality is not selfish. Only when we find real love, peace, harmony, and happiness within, can we share these gifts with others.

My spirituality blesses the world around me.

THINK ON THESE THINGS

The Christian Bible tells us to think about things which are true, noble, right, pure, lovely, praiseworthy, and honorable. The teachings of the Buddha advise "Right Mindfulness." Prophets, philosophers, and spiritual leaders from all times and traditions have told of the power of thought.

We may believe we have little control over all the information bombarding us every day. But when we take responsibility for what we think about, we can choose not to let negatives influence us from any source—other people, the media, and even our own memories and imaginations.

We can replace our frightening, depressing, worrysome, hostile, doubt-filled, and negative thoughts with happy, hopeful, inspiring, and uplifting ones. We can discover the transformational power of positive thinking.

I choose to think about hopeful, peaceful, loving things.

LOVING OURSELVES

Loving ourselves may be the hardest lesson we have to learn. It means letting go of believing we have to be perfect, and accepting ourselves as we are right now. It means giving ourselves whatever we need to grow.

Loving ourselves means forgiving ourselves for all our past mistakes. Forgiving doesn't mean approving, it means *understanding*. It means facing the realities of our lives without judgments.

Only when we learn to love ourselves can we begin to move foward with hope and joy. We can start by *acting as if* we love ourselves. Every day we can repeat such affirmations as "I love myself" and "I forgive myself for all my mistakes," even if we don't feel we really mean them yet. We can treat ourselves as we would treat a beloved friend.

I love myself.

OUR TRUE IDENTITY

When we look for spirituality within ourselves, we are not seeing ourselves as gods. Only the ego can imagine itself as a god or wish to be all-powerful. When we find our spiritual identity, we know it as our connection to a Power greater than ourselves.

It is important for us to discover this spiritual identity or we will only see ourselves as our body and ego. Identifying only with our outer image can lead us to an endless treadmill of searching for happiness where it can never be found, and trying to control what we can never control.

With humility, we can think of our spirit as the highest, best part of ourselves. Our true spiritual self is our Higher Power's gift to us.

Through my real spiritual identity, I reach toward God.

SLEEP

Our bodies require sleep to repair and rebuild themselves. But our minds and spirits also use sleep to refresh themselves and, sometimes, to communicate with us in dreams.

Just before we go to sleep and when we first awaken are often the best times for prayer and meditation because our conscious minds are most relaxed and least resistant. We can turn over any problems or worries we have to our Higher Power then. Often, an answer will come to us in a dream, or we'll wake up with a fresh idea or perspective on the situation. While our conscious minds sleep, we automatically get out of God's way and let the answers flow.

In the morning, we can take a moment before getting up, and, in a state of deep relaxation, thank our Higher Power and ask for help with the day ahead.

While I sleep, my Higher Power answers my prayers.

BEING

We're usually so busy *doing* things, that we're unaware of *being*. We may think we're being a wife or husband, mother or father, son or daughter, worker or boss, buyer or seller, or even man or woman. But these are all things we are *doing*.

In our daily meditation, we try to let go of doing—or even thinking about doing—anything. We open ourselves up to experiencing our *be-ing*. We are not being anything—the *be-ing* has no object. We are just *be-ing*—fully experiencing ourselves in the present moment.

The value of just *be-ing* lies in changing our perspective on ourselves. Without all our labels and roles, we can find our spiritual selves more easily. We return from our experience of *be-ing* with greater serenity, which enhances all of the things we *do*.

I take time each day to experience my be-ing.

THE LIGHT WITHIN

As we close our eyes and relax our bodies, breathing deeply and slowly, we can imagine that deep inside us there is a still, peaceful lake. The water is as smooth as glass, reflecting a perfect blue sky. As we stay with this calm, tranquil image, we notice a twinkling of sunlight on the water. It is like a beautiful, sparkling star. This light spreads slowly and gently across the water, until the entire lake becomes a glorious bright light. The warmth of this light radiates throughout our bodies. It feels gentle, loving, and healing. We are bathed in this beautiful light.

We can recall this light when we feel lost, confused, angry, tired, fearful, or whenever we wish. It will always bring us love, peace, and tranquility.

The light within me fills me with perfect love and serenity.